# Arcadia, One Mile

*Poetry*
Walking Under Water
Tenants of the House
Poems, Golders Green
A Small Desperation
Funland and Other Poems
Collected Poems 1948–1976
Way Out in the Centre
Ask the Bloody Horse
White Coat, Purple Coat: Poems 1948–1988
Remembrance of Crimes Past
On the Evening Road

*Editor*
The Hutchinson Book of Post-War British Poets
Twentieth Century Anglo-Welsh Poetry

*Plays*
The View from Row G.
(*Three plays*: House of Cowards,
The Dogs of Pavlov, Pythagoras Smith)

*Novels*
Ash on a Young Man's Sleeve
Some Corner of an English Field
O. Jones, O. Jones
There Was a Young Man from Cardiff

*Other Prose*
Medicine on Trial
A Poet in the Family (*Autobiography*)
A Strong Dose of Myself (*Confessions, Stories,
    Essays*)
Journals from the Ant Heap
Intermittent Journals

# Arcadia,
# One Mile

*Dannie Abse*

*Debora's*

*via*

*Lynn, Claudia and*
*Marilyn.*
*for our dear friend*

*Dannie Abse.*

*Hutchinson*
LONDON

1 3 5 7 9 10 8 6 4 2

This edition first published in 1998 by
Hutchinson
Random House (UK) Limited
20 Vauxhall Bridge Road, London SW1V 2SA

Random House Australia (Pry) Limited
20 Alfred Street, Milsons Point, Sydney,
New South Wales 2061, Australia

Random House New Zealand Limited
18 Poland Road, Glenfield,
Auckland 10, New Zealand

Random House South Africa (Pty) Ltd
Endulini, 5A Jubilee Road,
Parktown 2193, South Africa

A CiP record for this book is available
from the British Library

Papers used by Random House UK Limited are natural,
recyclable products made from wood grown in sustainable
forests. The manufacturing processes conform to the
environmental regulations of the country of origin.

ISBN 0 09 173455 X

Typeset in Bembo by MATS, Southend-on-Sea, Essex
Printed and bound in Great Britain by
Mackays of Chatham PLC

Acknowledgements are owed to the B.B.C. for new poems broadcast during the 1996 Edinburgh Festival and *Stanza on Stage*.

Some poems were first published in the following English and Welsh periodicals and books: *Acumen, The Author, Drawing Down The Moon* (Seren), *The Jewish Chronicle, The Jewish Quarterly, The Lancet, London Magazine, The New Statesman, New Writing 5 and 6* (British Council), *Orbis 100, Planet, P.N.Review, The Poetry Review, The Poet's View,* (Headland), *Poetry Wales, Stand, Trying the Line,* (Gomer) and *Welsh Retrospective* (Seren).

Others appeared in American magazines: *The Georgia Review, The Iowa Review, Michigan Quarterly Review, Pivot* (New York) and *TriQuarterly* (Chicago).

The second section of the poem 'Domestic' is a variation of some lines in 'The Claim' by T. Carmi. See *Selected Poems*, T. Carmi and Dan Pagis, Penguin Modern European Poets, 1976.

# Contents

# O Taste and See

Because of a kiss on the forehead
in the long Night's infirmary,
through the red wine let light shine deep.

Because of the thirtysix just men
that so stealthily roam this earth
raise high the glass and do not weep.

Who says the world is not a wedding?
Couples, in their oases, lullabye.
Let glass be full before they sleep.

Toast all that which seems to vanish
like a rainbow stared at, those bright
truant things that will not keep;

and ignorance of the last night
of our lives, its famished breathing.
Then, in the red wine, taste the light.

# The Maestro

'I'll portray you with flutes, oboes and harp.'
So Schumann to Clara. As I would you.

Now, in this front room of a tree-repeated street,
I practise mere stumbling tunes. But the maestro
behind me, in the mirror, my discreet double,
plays your music's parables flawlessly,
Schumann-like, strange and tragical and sweet.

# At the Albert Hall

Anarchic dissonances first, so that
somewhere else a lonely scarecrow shivers
in a winter field. A mortician's crow
perches on its head. It begins to snow.
They bring the scarecrow indoors. They feed it
with phosphorus so it should glow at night.
A great orchestra's tuning-up is ghost talk.

The wand! Then the sudden tamed silence of
a cemetery. Who dares to blackly cough?
Threatened, the conductor raises both arms,
an invisible gun pressed to his back.
Listen. And they speak of the sweet psalmist
of Israel, of 200 loaves of bread
and of 100 bundles of raisins.

# The Musical Express

A boy like you, he had said (1946)
will end up on the Musical Express.

What did that Swiss Cottage refugee,
that graphologist from Vienna
who had escaped the sealed wagons
mean?

I looked at my own handwriting
as if it were a mirror,
saw only a frosted window.

Did he refer merely to symphonic music's
totalitarian finale,
how loudly it accelerates towards silence?

My allegro days are here now:
one morning vast cloudless heaven
unautographed
full of someone else's Forever;
the next, when I blink,
another day, another season,
the stern modesties of a Welsh sky.

You'll end up, son, on the Musical Express.

Rain or shine, days track by so fast now
I can't read the stations' names
that I'm passing through.

One long slanting afternoon,
travelling in the U.S.A. when I was young,
first I saw a road sign:
ARCADIA, ONE MILE,
then a line of automobiles
all with headlights on,
coming towards me at mourning pace.

Et in Arcadia ego.

Consider the eyes of baby Hitler
new born, a colourless blue,
that graphologist had said.
Like yours were. Like mine.

Why should I tell you more?
Some touch wood and some stone touches
and a fool is his own informer,
autobiography a form of suicide.

He spoke adagio, that survivor,
– adagio molto espressivo –
and I, so lucky, knew how
the half-sleeping mind has many caves
and a man's country, too, is his fate.

# Photograph and White Tulips

A little nearer please. And a little nearer
we move to the window, to the polished table.
Objects become professional: mannequins
preening themselves before an audience. Only
the tulips, self-absorbed, ignore the camera.

All photographs flatter us if we wait
long enough. So we awkwardly Smile please
while long-necked tulips, sinuous out of the vase,
droop over the polished table. They're entranced
by their own puffed and smudgy reflections.

Hold it! Click. Once more! And we smile again
at one who'll be irrevocably absent.
Quick. Be quick! the tulips, like swans, will dip
their heads deep into the polished table
frightening us. Thank you. And we turn thinking,

What a fuss! Yet decades later, dice thrown,
we'll hold it, thank you, this fable of gone
youth (was that us?) and we shall smile please
and come a little nearer to the impetuous
once-upon-a-time that can never be twice.

(Never never be twice!) Yet we'll always recall
how white tulips, quick quick, changed into swans
enthralled, drinking from a polished table.
As for those white petals, they'll never fall
in that little black coffin now carrying us.

# The Boasts of
# Hywel ab Owain Gwynedd

*(12th century)*


Sunday, skilled in zealous verse I praise the Lord.
Monday, I sing in bed to my busty Nest,
'Such whiteness you are, pear blossom must be jealous.'
Tuesday, scholar Gwladus. Not to love her is a sin.
*My* couplets she pigeon-coos when I thrust to woo her
till her pale cheeks flush like rosy apple skin.
Wednesday, Generys. Dry old hymns I steal to please her.
Then with passion fruit in season I kneel to ease her.
Thursday, Hunydd, no hesitating lady, she.
One small cherry-englyn and she's my devotee.
Friday, worried Hawis, my epic regular.
She wants no baby, she's gooseberry vehement
till sugared by my poetry of endearment.
Saturday, I score and score. One tidy eulogy
and I'm away – I can't brake –- through an orchard
I adore. O sweet riot of efflorescence,
let her name be secret for her husband's sake,
my peach of a woman, my vegetarian diet.

O tongue, lick up juices of the fruit. O teeth
– I've all of mine – be sure my busy tongue keeps quiet.

# Lament of Heledd

*(based on a fragment of a 9th century Welsh saga poem)*

## I

I had four brothers. A pike upholds the head
of noble Cynddylan. The corn is red.

I had four brothers. Cynon and Gwiawn
butchered in the straw, their swords not drawn.

I had four  brothers. Vague, hesitant Gwyn
last to fall. Through his neck a javelin.

When will this brute night end? Where shall I go?
Morning's mortuary will be kitchen for the crow.

## II

Cynddylan's Hall is dark tonight.
The stone stairs lead nowhere. No candle glows
behind the lower then the higher windows.

Cynddylan's Hall is dark tonight
and dark the smoke rising from its ruin.
Slain, slain, are Cynddylan and all our kin.

Cynddylan's Hall is dark tonight,
its great roof burnt down, I can see the stars.
Curse those Englishmen, their bloody wars.

Cynddylan's Hall is dark tonight.
No orison is wailed to harp or lute.
O  ghost brothers, your sister's destitute.

Cynddylan's Hall is dark tonight,
its silence outrageous. I shall go mad.
I smell skeletons. O blood of my blood.

Cynddylan's Hall is dark tonight.
Should I live on? I am no heroine.
O  Cynddylan, Cynon, Gwiawn, and Gwyn.

# Welsh Valley Cinema, 1930s

In The Palace of the slums,
from the Saturday night pit,
from an unseen shaft of darkness
I remember it: how, first, a sound
took wing grandly; then the thrill
of a fairground sight – it rose,
lordly stout thing, boasting
a carnival of gaudy-bright,
changing colours while wheezing out
swelling rhonchi of musical asthma.

I hear it still, played with panache
by renowned gent, Cathedral Jones,
'When the Broadway Baby Says Goodnight
it's Early in the Morning' – then he and it
sank to disappear, a dream underground.

Later, those, downstairs, gobbing silicosis
(shoeless feet on the mecca carpet),
observed a miracle – the girl next door,
a poor ragged Goldilocks,
dab away her glycerine tears
to kiss cuff-linked Cary Grant
under an elegance of chandeliers.
(No flies on Cary. No holes in *his* socks.)

And still the Woodbine smoke swirled on
in the opium beam of the operator's box
till THE END – of course, upbeat.
Then from The Palace, the damned Fall,
the glum, too silent trooping out
into the trauma of paradox:
the familiar malice of the dreary,
unemployed, gas-lamped street
and the striking of the small Town's clocks.

# Sixth-Form Poet

When my acne almost cleared
I fell in love with humankind.
I wanted to requisition Poetry,
a revolution in my mind.

To the barricades not the court,
my gorgeous rage would console.
Though love be blind it sees
with the optic nerve of the soul.

Poetry is written in the brain
but the brain is bathed in blood.
I sang no praises for the King,
I, laureate to Robin Hood.

# A Political Prisoner

'Franco could have freed Miguel Hernandez from prison.
How could a shepherd boy used to living in the open air
live seven years in prison. He got T.B. His execution was
carried out by Tuberculosis.' Neruda

1

The noise of many knuckles on metal,
we do not hear it.
There is lightning when we are asleep
and thunder that does not speak;
there are guitars without strings
and nightingales with tongues of glass.

Yet even if we imagine it,
the metal sound of bolts shut to,
then feet stamping down echoing corridors,
what can we do who stroll on easy grass,
who smile back at the gracious and the
goodlooking?

Righteous the rhetoric of indignation,
but protesting poems, like the plaster angels,
are impotent. They commit no crimes,
they pass no laws; they grant amnesty
only to those who, in safety, write them.

2

Shepherd from the village, Orihuela,
who, whistling, could mimic different birds,
who, by day, would count the cabra,
by night, from the hills, the straying stars,
you opened your eyelids noiselessly,
found you were sitting, hunched in a cell.
You howled, hurled a bucket at the bars.

Far from the villanelle of nightingales
or the sexual moan in the throat of doves,
they handed you a bible, remarked slyly,
'Poet, feel at home.' Then Hell's Time
seemed to strike its palindrome note
and you knew you would perish in that cell.
'Flesh falls off gradually,
bones collapse suddenly,' you wrote.

3

Within the towering walls of every grey jail,
especially at night, the desire to escape
from the clock's small thefts. Maybe for you, too,
once, after lights out, it was carnival time:
drums beating, somersaulting clowns, men on stilts,
each wearing a bull's mask meant to chill,
and lewd codpieces of unnatural size.
Then the coloured carts and their pretty lanterns,
marching girls in skimpy skirts, bare lifting thighs,
fire-swallowers and those with a juggling skill.

Surely they came, moving pictures, floating
like pointillist dust in substantial moonbeams,
through your cramped cell – though vanishing at dawn
when all the birds that ever were, near and remote,
did not sweetly sing or corvine croak; but coughed,
as you did, spills of bacilli and blood.

The stinking vultures! The pterodactyls!

'You threw me a lemon, it was sour,' you wrote.

# C'est La Vie Politique

When promised
a subtle perfume,
tactful dilutions
of musk, civet, ambergris,

expect 'a human error',
a veritable gasworks.
Dry in the polluted air
plain $H_2S$.

When promised
a hundred piece orchestra –
Berlioz, Mahler –
a tune on a comb.

When a Queen's diamond,
a snail's shell;
when a King's golden crown,
a funny paper hat.

Consider Mr Maltby,
fancy tailor, who agreed
a suicide pact
with his wife.

She did not falter;
he was unable.
He propped her up
naked in the bath.

Night after night
brought lit candles
into that bathroom
where he quietly dined,

faithfully choosing
her favourite dishes,
fish mainly – turbot, trout –
gently removing the bones.

# Refugee

What is the name of your country?
 Its frontiers keep changing.
What is the Capital of your country?
 The town where blood issued
 through the cold and hot water taps.
What is your National Anthem?
 The ancient fugue of screams.
Who are your compatriots?
 The crippled, the groping blinded,
 the wan dead not yet in their dungeons.
Who is your leader?
 Death's trumpet-tongued fool.
What is the name of your son?
 Despair.
What is the name of your daughter?
 Derangement.
Why is your husband not with you?
 He raised high the pleading
 white flag of surrender.

# A Heritage

A heritage of a sort.
A heritage of comradeship and suffocation.

The bawling pit-hooter and the god's
explosive foray, vengeance, before retreating
to his throne of sulphur.

Now this black-robed god of fossils
and funerals,
petrifier of underground forests
and flowers,
emerges with his grim retinue
past a pony's skeleton, past human skulls,
into his half-propped up, empty, carbon colony.

Above, on the brutalised,
unstitched side of a Welsh mountain,
it has to be someone from somewhere else
who will sing solo

not of the marasmus of the Valleys,
the pit-wheels that do not turn,
the pump-house abandoned;

nor of how, after a half-mile fall
regiments of miners' lamps
no longer, midge-like,
rise and slip and bob.

Only someone uncommitted,
someone from somewhere else,
panorama-high on a coal-tip,
may jubilantly laud
the re-entry of the exiled god
into his shadowless kingdom.

He, drunk with methane,
raising a man's femur like a sceptre;
she, his ravished queen,
admiring the blood-stained black roses
that could not thrive on the plains of Enna.

# Altercation in Splott

Before the frosted window is shattered
immigrant, touch stone and be lucky.

Widower, Sunil, calls most men, 'Sir.'
Hindu pacifist, chanter of prayers.

Cold and cloned, the next door room to his:
bed, chair, threadbare carpet, vertical

fat coffin with a keyhole in it,
damp stain of almost Wales on the wall,

inert with the slow interminable
silence of a broken radio

till volcano-loud, football hooligan,
Darren Jones, big-boots in. Me? Racialist?

Nah. Politics is shit, mun. On the stairs
I smiles back at the Paki, see.

But rust sleeps within the iron.
One night, pub closed, Darren's jugular.

Paki, you wanker, stop chantin', Christ!
Nothin' much, see. Bust 'is 'ead in a bit

that's all. No shit under the door like.
Righteous as a Town Hall, Darren Jones.

One winter week's notice for bleak Sunil.
Never complain to a blue-eyed landlord.

Ice is on the pond. Swan is on the snow.
But far from the neighbourhood of parks,

Sunil, long-armed, suitcase in each hand,
treads past the depot on pavements' linen,

seems, in sleet–mist, more a conjuration
than a man. Indian out of season.

Sir, stone falls on jug: woe.
Sir, jug falls on stone: woe.

# Assimilation

Even the Sodomites, I said, would allow
distraught refugees into their desert city,
provide them with a Sodom-made bed.

But strangers too tall, it must be admitted,
had their legs chopped off; and nationalistic Sods
heaved at heads and feet of those too small
till beds and bodies beautifully fitted.

# Souls

'After the last breath, eyelids must be closed
quickly. For eyes are windows of the soul
– that shy thing which is immortal. And none
should see its exit vulnerably exposed,'

proclaimed the bearded man on Yom Kippur.
Grown-ups believed in the soul. Otherwise
why did grandfather murmur the morning prayer,
'Lord, the soul Thou hast given me is pure'?

Near the kitchen door where they notched my height
a mirror hung. There I saw the big eyes
of a boy. I could not picture the soul
immaterial and immortal. A cone of light?

Those two black zeros the soul's windows? Daft!
Later, at medical school, I learnt of
the pineal gland, its size a cherry-stone,
vestige of the third eye, and laughed.

But seven colours hide in light's disguise
and the blue sky's black. No wonder Egyptians
once believed, in their metamorphosis,
souls soared, became visible: butterflies.

Now old, I'm credulous. Superstition clings.
After the melting eyes and devastation
of Hiroshima, they say butterflies, crazed,
flew about, fluttering soundless things.

# My Neighbour, Itzig

My neighbour, Itzig,
has gone queer with religion.
Yesterday he asked me
who named the angels!

Today his dog is barking and barking.

But like music that's ceased
in an adjoining room
Itzig is not here.
He is nowhere else, either.

Itzig, listen, your dog needs a walk.

But Itzig is droning on and on
– open the window, someone –
a prayer archaic and musty
and full of O.

His sad feet are on this earth,
his happy head is elsewhere
among the configuration
of the 7 palaces of light.

Come back, Itzig, your dog needs feeding.

But Itzig quests for the 8th colour.
His soul is cartwheeling, he's far
from the barely manageable
drama of the Present Tense.

Come back, Itzig, your dog needs water.

But Itzig follows, with eyes closed,
the footsteps of the sages
Amora and Rehumai
who never existed.

# A Letter from Ogmore-by-Sea

Goodbye, 20th Century.
What should I mourn?
Hiroshima? Auschwitz?
Our friend, Carmi, said,
'Thank forgetfulness
else we could not live;
thank memory
else we'd have no life.'

Goodbye, 20th Century.
What shall I celebrate?
Darling, I'm out of date:
even my nostalgia
is becoming history.
Those garish, come-on posters
outside a cinema,
announce the Famous
I've never heard of.
So many other friends, too,
now like Carmi, have joined
a genealogy of ghosts.

But here, this mellow evening,
on these high cliffs I look down
to read the unrolling
holy scrolls of the sea. They are
blank. The enigma is alive
and, for the Present, I boast,
thumbs in lapels, I survive.

Delightful Eros
still hauls Reason along
zig-zag on a taut leash.
I'm still unsettled by
the silence in framed pictures,
foreground and background;
or the mastery of music
over mind. And I hail
the world within a word.
I do not need to be
a fabulist like Iolo
who, from this same coast,
would see seven sails
where there was but one.

Goodbye, 20th Century,
your trumpets and your drums,
your war-wounds still unhealed.
Goodbye, I–must–leave–you–Dolly,
goodbye Lily Marlene.
Has the Past always a future?
Will there always be
a jackboot on the stair,
a refugee to roam?
A man with no roots is lost
like the darkness in the forest
and it costs 100 years
for a hiding place
to become a home.

Now secular strangers come
sealed in Fords and Nissans,
a congregation of cars,
to this opening estuary
so various, so beautiful, so old.
The tide is out.
And from the reeled –
in sea – not from
the human mind's vexed fathoms –
the eternal, murderous,
fanged Tusker Rock is revealed.

# An Interrupted Letter

In this room's winterlight the travail of
a letter to a new widow. Solemn,
the increasing enterprise of age.
I stutter. Consoling words come slow,
seem false, as if spoken on a stage.
It would be easier to send flowers.

I think of her closing her husband's eyelids
and I look up. Siberian snow hesitated,
then parachuted into our garden
for hours, confiscating yesterday's
footprints. Shall I send flowers?

But now my wife, unaware in the far kitchen,
suddenly sings, captivating me,
my pen mid-air above a muffled page.

When we were young, tremulant with Spring,
often off-key she'd sing her repertoire –
dateless folk songs, dance tunes dated.
In her Pears-suds bath I'd hear her,
in the Morris Minor with our kids.

I must return to my hiemal letter.
Sing on love, as once you did, sing and sing
for past youth, for hungers unabated.

# Useful Knowledge

Shy Colin, the most silent of men
despite his ammunition of facts.
He'd bomb them out at dinner parties
before signing off from conversation.

'The mastrich tree, as you probably know,
is brown, resinous, and most fragrant.'
'Volapuk? Nobody speaks it now.
Lost its one thousand, five hundred words.'

At Anne's, he said, 'Tortoises often die
from diphtheria.' At our place, he told us
'Lake Titicaca's half the size of Wales –
half's in Bolivia, half in Peru.'

Last April , when his two year old son
lay big-eyed in The Royal Infirmary,
Colin heard the consultant whisper
to his Registrar, 'Nieman-Pick Disease.'

Colin closed his eyes, cried out shrilly,
'A genetically determined disorder
where splenectomy is palliative.
Death occurs quite early during childhood.'

# Alzheimer's

Absolutely nothing
8 jars of nothing
And 1 jar of barley sugar
    2 jars of acid drops
    3 jars of chocolate drops
    4 jars of liquorice allsorts
    5 jars of mintoes
    6 jars of humbugs
    7 jars of bulls' eyes.

An old-age adagio, cello-sad.
Suspicions, accusations,
whisperings of the profane,
the enthronement of doubt.
Then a turning back,
light blue, dark blue, purple,
to the bleak mechanism.
Aphasia, agnosia,
a blank 75″ record, black
like the far farmhouse
that merges with
night-surrounding fields
when the electric
in the high bedroom
at last goes out.

And 7 jars of bulls' eyes
    6 jars of humbugs
    5 jars of mintoes
    4 jars of liquorice allsorts
    3 jars of chocolate drops
    2 jars of acid drops
    1 jar of barley sugar
    8 jars of nothing
    absolutely nothing

# Child Drawing in a Hospital Bed

Any child can open wide
the occult doors of a colour
naively to call, 'Who's there?'
For this sick girl drawing
outstep invisible ones
imprisoned everywhere.
Wasp on a windowpane.

Darkest tulip her head bends,
face white as leukaemia,
till the prince in his tower,
on parole from a story,
descends by royal crayon
and, thrilled, stays half an hour.
Wasp on a windowpane.

Birds of Rhiannon, pencilled,
alight to wake the dead –
they do not sing, she rubs them out,
they smudge into vanishings,
they swoop to Nowhere
as if disturbed by a shout.
Wasp on a windowpane.

Omens. Wild astrologies whirl:
sun and moon begin to soar.
Unlikely that maroon sky
green Christmas trees fly through
– doctors know what logic's for.
Tell me, what is magic for?
Wasp on a windowpane.

34

Now penal-black she profiles
four eerie malformed horses,
nostrils tethered to the ground.
Unperturbed, the child attends
for one to uplift its neck
and turn its death's head round.
Wasp on a windowpane.

# Thomas Girtin's
## 'The White House'

Something odd about the house – so luminous
as if a truant god were resting there.

And those daffodil-bordered clouds seem intent
to spill but will, of course, never. Their oblique
presentiments of rain, their pollutions of smoke
behind, above, a huge icon of a windmill.

Though such painted scenes reject the future,
and quarrel with the ghost of Heraclitus,
now, sleep-walking into Girtin's numinous
mastery of a moment, I want narrative.

I want to forecast what the weather will bring
but all the clocks within that spotlit house,
the effulgent white house on the promontory,
have stopped at the mood of eternal evening.

The contrary sky cannot play its mobiles;
no chill wind can turn around the cross
of this indisposed windmill or stir the still
waters, the fishing boats, their capsized doubles.

I want to smell something more than paint. Loud Life!
its shyest flowers that must be held so close
before their scent is known. Life's armpits, too!
I'm troubled by the silence of this river view.

I want to trick the picture fast-forward,
shake it like a watch to make Time's nothings tick;
let the yawning god quit the house perplexed;
the complacent winds to be vexed again;

anaesthetised fishermen to go home unsurprised
to empty firegrates or expectant wives.

# The Stonebreaker

Dear Inchbold,
                    I want you to know about this.

23 miles from London I was walking
with Black Spot when I lingered to gaze at
a steep scarp of the chalky Downs.
I gazed and gazed until I seemed to stand
                    just outside Eden.

Faraway, the beech trees in their summer
magnificence while, nearby, there happened to be
a pile of stones and a barely living tree.
It sprang out of a dead one.

                    Oh Inchbold,
do you believe in the Resurrection?

Remember mild Tom, the model who died,
the one who resembled my young brother?
Suddenly, from nowhere, he appeared
and, with a noiseless hammer, struck the stones.
He did not look pathetic like the Stonebreaker
portrayed by Henry Wallis but wore fake,
unsoiled, peasant's clothes.

                    Before I could speak
a bullfinch alighted on a high branch
of the strange, frail tree and Tom vanished.

You doubt what I saw? I doubt what I saw.
So much is mirage and shadow. The law
of gravity asserts itself in my mind.
I know the far hills are not really blue,
that sunlight does not truly paint the grass
an indistinct yellow. Love, itself, errs.
A child's swift daubs on paper are not Art
though the mother may think so.

         Oh Inchbold,
did I see what I saw? Tom breaking stones?

  I beg you, tell no-one of this. You know
how some believe we artists are crazy!
Besides, I may paint this experience though
Ruskin says mine is mirror's work not man's.
Write me soon. Your loving friend,

        John Brett.

# In the Welsh National Museum

*(To Josef Herman)*

Josef, in your thaumaturgic studio,
long live cobalt blue and brown!
Autumn is your season,
twilight is your hour.

Now, in my hometown, you, spooky,
conjure up, abracadabra,
this melancholy impostor
who steals my name.

Is he listening to someone
beyond the picture's frame,
playing a Chopin piano
of autumnal unhappiness?

Josef, this other is not me.
This golem hardly looks like me.
Is this your unbegotten brother
lost in menstrual blood?

If so, his passport (forged)
would have been Polish,
his exile inevitable,
his wound undescribable.

Look! My best brown coat
not yet patched at the elbow,
my cobalt blue shirt
not yet frayed at the collar.

As if challenged he, dire,
(Passport? Colour of wound?)
stares back – that look of loss –
at whomsoever stares at him.

Or across at Augustus John's
too respectable W. H. Davies,
at prettified Dylan Thomas
whose lips pout for a kiss.

Infelicitous! Wrong! Impostors
spellbound, enslaved in their world,
with no *emeth* on their foreheads,
without speech, without pneuma.

But the Welsh say, 'Whoever stares long
at his portrait will, with dismay, see
the devil.' So who's wearing my clothes?
Josef, I know your magic. I'll not stay.

# Deaf Men Singing

*(To Gillian)*

Most poems, like golems, turn to dust at dawn
but you hallow the coarse endeavour, attend
the awkward, the not winging, the also-rans;
cheer Z because it's last; salute deaf men singing
who feel a piano's wood to hear its song,
myopic painters, their details clearly wrong,
their vast perspectives to a No-Man's Past.

Inhuman angels may command perfection
but the hollow circle drawn by Giotto
would have been more genial if hand had wavered.
So you commend sweet error, would not mend
the nervous junction, convert the letter O
to Death's infrangible and favoured number,
with its unseen beginning, no evident end.

# Domestic

*To His Wife*

You need not be cross, why are you
cross-examining me?

By Ishara, queen of the oaths,
hear me out
— let's contend no more, love —

by Ishtar of Nineveh,
by Ishtar of Hattarina,

— do not shout,
what so wild as words are? —

by the hypertensive lord of Wars,
by St Elmo and by Santa Claus,

after the doors of dawn re-opened
— let's cease our battling, love —

I was still bloody-well rattling
bars of a stationary lift
between electrically-lit, empty floors.

*To His Friend's Wife*

No letters, no photos, no keepsake.

No whistling of a coded tune,
no signals of lover to his lass.

I think you're glad I didn't
when the sea surrendered to the moon.

No scratches, no love-bites, no heartache.

I think I'm glad I didn't
when the church clock tolled the hour.

Your ring shone muffled gold not wanton brass.

Judgement Night we'll not shuffle
to the bench, bent, crass, trembling,
beg pardon, your honour.

We'll stand there upright, alas.

# New Granddaughter

You don't know the score, what's you, what's not.
Remote ancestors return you can't disown.
This prelude, this waiting for an encore.

Is that raised hand yours, this wind-pecked morning?
Enigmatic trees, askew, shake above the pram.
All's perplexity, green reverie, shadowland.

But why this grandfatherly spurt of love?
Your skin is silk, your eyes suggest they're blue.
I bend to smell small apricots and milk.

Did I dream that legend of the Angel
who falls to touch each baby's fontanelle
and wipe out racial memory, leaving *déjà vu*?

I'm confessing! Your newness, petite, portends
my mortality – a rattle for you, the bell for me.
Hell, I'm old enough to mutter blessings.

The determinates of the clock increase.
Sometimes you close your eyes noiselessly, turn
your head, listening to music that has ceased.

# Presences

I'm halted by the unintentional
honeyed malice of mementos:
this awkward night-school painting
by my genial father-in-law;
this vast desk my mother fussed
to give me. 'Fit for an emperor!'

And here's another hook to chin:
a door opens in the next room
and I hear a snatch of Gershwin –
that tune our car-bound family used
to sing. On music's heartless beat
my keen dead come marching in.

O button-holing familiars,
your blurs I sense, your ashes I taste.
So much I owe, so much forgotten
that I owe. But now dear ghosts go
that I may live. Be brief guests.
Leave with a burglar's haste.

The future's future is another place
where other absences will sting; where
some unfocussed progeny perhaps
will summon me, stumbling on
some inherited thing or, less likely,
reading this poem, maybe!

# Last Lunch

*In memory of David Wright*

That last late lunch we had in Soho
you spoke of friends who had gone before,
edgy prisoners of poetry.

Would readers forget their astute verse–skill,
Jock Graham, Tom Blackburn, Stevie,
who taking the maverick route

from a poisoned tree made a table
and, at that table, ate its fruit?

Then you said, 'My turn, Dannie',
reaching for the bill.

# The Expert

Sir, item 66
is not, repeat is not
a fragment of the Berlin Wall.

As an expert I can vouch
it comes from Greece.
I have smelt it.
It is a fragment of a boulder.
I have felt its silence.

Sisyphus, very old,
lost his oxygen
at the summit of the mountain,
suffered a coronary,

let go,
and the boulder bounced down
on rocks, down,
frightening a settled eagle
below.

The eagle flapped,
beat dust out of its wings.
The boulder, down down, crashed
out of sight.

The eagle rose up, high,
drifted silently
around and around
the mountain top.

# Why Angels Disappeared

When first the celestial orchestra played
decorously the angels began to dance.

This was the time when the moon unmuzzled
glowed twice more luminously than now.

But wanton Azazel, the angel of Vice,
unhooked his nice masterpiece wings, displayed,

enticed daft angels to swig double-strength nectar,
deft angels to juggle the fruits of Paradise.

Hallelujah! Hallelujah! That unquiet night
(such an orgy) half the angels got laid

and their pet unicorns ran riot, began to bite,
called for pale maidens to make life rosier.

Their randy horns grew and grew. Some howled at
the moon, some crapped on the ambrosia.

Soon the Archangel's police arrived, blew
whistles for music to cease, moonlight to fade

and foolishly fed the frenetic unicorns
tinned human flesh, calming pesticides.

Later, the angels ate all the unicorns,
suffered CJD. Not one of them survived.

# The Arrival and Departure of Adam and Eve at Dover

## I

At the gate, expelled from the fable
of the East, the man's profile turned towards
the ullulating distraught woman.

And behind this couple now stumbling forward
– she half-bent over in her weeping –
the distant blitz–light of an angel.

## II

So many thousands of centuries passed
and, in their innocence, new friends eased them
of the bdellium, the onyx stone
and the little gold acquired in Havilah.

So many more miles of thorns and thistles,
so many more winters howled away
before they came, at last, penniless,
to the alerted paparazzi at Dover.

The fuss! The fuss! The woman moaned on,
inconsolable, but the man seemed composed
until secular officials decreed
they faced no danger in their native country.

The Home Secretary (appealed to) said,
'At the end of the day' and 'God is merciful'.
Ceremonious duty done the two
'economic migrants' were repatriated.

On TV newsreels see them stepping from
a police van, discharged from this little world,
this scepter'd isle, this other Eden,
still in disgrace, coats over their heads.

# Soho: Saturday Night

Always Cain, anonymous amidst the poor,
Abel dead in his eye, and over his damned sore
a khaki muffler, loiters, a fugitive in Soho,
enters The Golden Calf Club and hears Esau,

dishevelled and drunk, cursing kith and kin.
'A mess of pottage!' Esau strokes an unshaven chin
and strikes a marble table-top. Then hairy hands
fidget dolefully, raise up a glass of gin.

Outside, Joseph, dyspnoeic, regards a star
convexing over Dean Street, coughs up a flower
from ruined lungs – rosy petals on his tongue –
recalls the Pit and wounds of many a colour.

Traffic lights change. With tapping white stick
a giant crosses the road between the frantic
taxis. A philistine pimp laughs. Dancing
in The Nude Show Delilah suddenly feels sick.

Ruth, too, the innocent, was gullibly led,
lay down half-clothed on a brassy railing bed
of Mr Boaz of Bayswater. Now, too late, weeps
antiseptic tears, wishes she were dead.

Who goes home? Nebuchadnezzar to the doss-
house where, all night, he'll turn and toss.
Lunchtime, in Soho Square, he munched the grass
and now he howls at strangers as they pass.

In Café Babylon, Daniel, interpreter of dreams,
listens to Belshazzar, a shy lad in his teens:
'A soiled finger moved across the lavatory wall.'
Growing up is not so easy as it seems.

Prophets, like tipsters, awaiting the Advent.
Beggar Job, under the flashing advertisement
for toothpaste, the spirochaete in his brain,
groans. Chalks a lurid picture on the pavement.

The Golden Calf closes. Who goes home? All
tourists to Nod, psalmists from their pub crawl;
they leave unshaved Soho to its dawn furnace
of affliction, its wormwood and its gall.

# No Lazarus

At the time of the Resurrection
not one person rose up
from the cemeteries of London.
But, at Marylebone Road,
a procession of clothed dummies
streamed out of Madame Tussaud's,
arms raised, wild, shouting Hallelujah.

The Archbishop of Canterbury
and other official sources
denied a computer error.

# Inscription on the Flyleaf of a Bible

*(For Larne)*

Doubting, read what this fabled history teaches,
how the firework, Imagination, reaches high
to dignify and sanctify.

You need not, granddaughter, be religious
to learn what Judges, Kings, Prophets, yield,
thought-lanterns for Life's darker field,
moral lies of piety and poetry.

You need not, granddaughter, hosanna heroes:
this wily shepherd, that bloodthirsty tough;
yet applaud the bulrush child
who, when offered gold, chose the coal.
Satisfied, the tyrant Pharaoh smiled,
did not see the pattern in the whole.

Forgive the triumphalism and the pride,
forego the curses and the ritual stuff.
You, older, I hope, will always side
with the enslaved and hunted,
deride the loud and lethal crowd
who vilify and simplify.

What is poetry but the first words
Adam, amazed, spoke to Eve?
On the first page of Genesis
hear the next to Nothing.
Later sound-effects, God off-stage, or theurgic stunts,
(water from a rock, a bush ablaze) might deceive
but bring ladders only to nerveless heaven.
Better to walk with Jephthah's luckless daughter
among real hills. And grieve.

Enjoy David's winging gifts to praise;
Solomon's rapturous serenade; also Job's
night-starred elegance of distress –
though such eloquence can bless,
indiscriminately, the last flags of the just
and the unjust on the barricade.

Read, granddaughter, these scandalous stories,
screaming Joseph in the pit of scorpions,
champion Goliath of course outclassed;
so many cubits of sorrow and delight,
so many visions of our ruffian Past.
They do not stale or fade
and may fortify and mollify.

# Events Leading to the Conception of Solomon, The Wise Child

And David comforted Bathsheba his wife, and went into her, and lay with her; and she bore a son, and he called his name Solomon: and the Lord loved him.

I

Are the omina favourable?
Scribes know the King's spittle,
even the most honoured
like Seraiah the Canaanite,
and there are those, addicted,
who inhale
            the smoke of burning papyrus.

So is the date-wine sour, the lemon sweet?
Who can hear the sun's furnace?

The shadow of some great bird
            drifts indolently
across the ochres and umbers
of the afternoon hills
            that surround Jerusalem.
Their rising contours, their heat-refracting
            undulations.

The lizard is on the ledges,
the snake is in the crevices.

It is where Time lives.

Below, within the thermals of the Royal
                City,
past the cursing camel driver,
past the sweating woman carrying water
                in a goatskin,
past the leper peeping through
                the lateral slats
of his fly-mongering latrine
to the walls of the Palace itself,
the chanting King is at prayer.

                Aha, aha,
attend to my cry, O Lord
who makest beauty
to be consumed away like a moth;
purge me with hyssop and I
                shall be clean.
Wash me and I shall be whiter
                than the blossom.
Blot out my iniquities.

Not yet this prayer,not yet
            that psalm.
It is where a story begins.
Even the bedouin beside their black tents
have heard the desert wind's rumour.
They ask:
            Can papyrus grow
where there is no marsh?
They cry:
            *Sopher yodea*
to the Scribe with two tongues,
urge him to tend his kingdom
of impertinence.


II

When the naked lady stooped to bathe
   in the gushings of a spring,
the voyeur on the tower roof
   just happened to be the King.


She was summoned to the Palace
   where the King displayed his charms;
he stroked the harp's glissandos,
   sang her a couple of psalms.


Majestic sweet-talk in the Palace
   – he name-dropped Goliath and Saul –
till only one candle-flame flickered
   and two shadows moved close on the wall.

Of course she hankered for the Palace.
    Royal charisma switched her on.
Her husband snored at the Eastern Front,
    so first a kiss, then scruples gone.

Some say, 'Sweet victim in the Palace,'
    some say, 'Poor lady in his bed.'
But Bathsheba's teeth like milk were white,
    and her mouth like wine was red.

David, at breakfast, bit an apple.
    She, playful, giggling, seized his crown,
then the apple-flesh as usual
    after the bite turned brown.

## III

In the kitchen, the gregarious, hovering flies
where the servants breakfast.
A peacock struts
            in its irradiance,
and is ignored.

On the stone floor and on the shelves
the lovely shapes of utensils,
great clay pots, many jugs of wine,
            many horns of oil,
the food-vessels and the feast-boards.

On the long table, butter of kine, thin loaves,
bowls of olives and griddle-cakes,
wattled baskets of summer fruit,
flasks of asses' milk and jars of honey.

What a tumult of tongues,
              the maids and the men,
the hewers of wood,
the drawers of water,
              the narrow-skulled
              and the wide-faced.
What a momentary freedom prospers,
              a detour from routine,
a substitute for mild insurrection.

They ask:
    In his arras-hung chamber
    did the King smell of the sheepcote?
    On the ivory bench, did he seat her
              on cushions?
    Did she lie on the braided crimson couch,
    beneath her head pillows of goat hair?

    Who saw him undo her raiments?
    Who overheard Uriah's wife,
    Bathsheba of the small voice,
              cry out?
    Was it a woman made love to
    or the nocturnal moan
              of the turtle dove?

Will the priest, Nathan, awaken
who, even in his sleep, mutters
             Abomination?

Now she who is beautiful to look upon
leaves furtively by a back door.
She will become a public secret.
She wears fresh garments of blue and purple,
the topaz of Ethiopia beneath her apparel.
But a wind gossips in the palm trees,
the anaphora of the wind
             in the fir-trees of Senir,
             in the cedars of Lebanon,
             in the oaks of Bashan.
It flaps the tents where Uriah, the Hittite,
is encamped with Joab's army
on the Eastern open fields.

Does purity of lust last one night only?
In the breakfasting kitchen, the peacock screams.

IV

The wind blows and the page turns over.
   Soon the King was reading a note.
Oh such excruciating Hebrew:
   'I've one in the bin,' she wrote.

Since scandal's bad for royal business
   the King must not father the child;
so he called Uriah from the front,
   shook his hand like a voter. Smiled.

Uriah had scorned the wind's whisper,
     raised his eyebrows in disbelief.
Still, here was the King praising his valour,
     here was the King granting him leave.

In uniform rough as a cat's tongue
     the soldier artlessly said,
'Hard are the stones on the Eastern Front,
     but, Sire, harder at home is my bed.'

Though flagons and goat-meat were offered
     the Hittite refused to go home.
He lingered outside the Palace gates,
     big eyes as dark as the tomb.

Silk merchants came and departed,
     they turned from Uriah appalled –
for the soldier sobbed in the stony heat,
     ignored his wife when she called;

sat down with his sacks, sat in the sun,
     sat under stars and would not quit,
scowled at the King accusingly
     till the King got fed up with it.

'Stubborn Uriah, what do you want?
     Land? Gold? Speak and I'll comply.'
Then two vultures creaked overhead
     to brighten the Hittite's eye.

'Death.' That's what he sought in the desert
   near some nameless stony track.
And there two vultures ate the soldier
   with a dagger in his back.

The widow was brought to the Palace,
   a Queen for the King-size bed,
and oh their teeth like milk were white,
   and their mouths like wine were red.

V

Should there be merriment at a funeral?
Stones of Jerusalem, where is your lament?
Should her face not have been leper-ashen?
Should she not have torn at her apparel
         bayed at the moon?
Is first young love
      always a malady?

When Uriah roared with the Captains of Joab,
      the swearing garrisons,
the dust leaping behind the chariots,
      the wagons, the wheels;
when his sword was unsheathed
amidst the uplifted trumpets
and the cacophony of donkeys;
when he was fierce as a close-up,
      huge with shield and helmet;
when his face was smeared with vermilion,
did she think of him less
      than a scarecrow in a field?

When she was more girl than woman
who built for her
            a house of four pillars?
When his foot was sore
            did she not dip it in oil?
When his fever seemed perilous
            did she not boil the figs?

When the morning stars sang together,
face to face, they sang together.
At night when she shyly stooped
            did he not boldly soar?

When, at midnight, the owl screeched
            who comforted her?
When the unclothed satyr danced
            in moonlight
who raised a handkerchief to her wide eyes?

When the archers practised
            in the green pastures
whose steady arm curled about her waist?

True love is not briefly displayed
like the noon glory of the fig marigold.

Return oh return
pigeons of memory to your homing land.

But the scent was only a guest
          in the orange tree.
The colours faded
          from the ardent flowers
not wishing to outstay their visit.

VI

The wind blows and the page turns over.
     To Bathsheba a babe was born.
Alas, the child would not feed by day,
     by night coughed like a thunderstorm.

'Let there be justice after sunset,'
     cried Nathan, the raging priest.
Once again he cursed the ailing child
     and the women's sobs increased.

So the skeletal baby sickened
     while the King by the cot-side prayed
and the insomniac mother stared
     at a crack in the wall afraid.

Nobody played the psaltery,
     nobody dared the gameboard.
The red heifer and doves were slaughtered.
     A bored soldier cleaned his stained sword.

Courtiers huddled in the courtyard,
     rampant their whisperings of malice.
The concubines strutted their blacks.
     The spider was in the Palace.

Soon a battery of doors in the Palace,
    soon a weird shout, 'The child is dead.'
Then Bathsheba's teeth like milk were white,
    and her eyes like wine were red.

Outside the theatre of the shrine
    David's penitent spirit soared
beyond the trapped stars. He wept. He danced
    the dance of death before the Lord.

That night the King climbed to her bedroom.
    Gently he coaxed the bereaved
and in their shared and naked suffering
    the wise child, love, was conceived.


*CODA*

Over the rocky dorsals of the hills
the pilgrim buses of April arrive,
one by one, into Jerusalem.

There was a jackal on the site
                of the Temple
before the Temple was built.

And stones. The stones only.

Are the omina favourable?
Will there be blood on the thorn bush?
Does smoke rising from the rubbish dump
          veer to the West or to the East?
So much daylight! So much dust!
This scribe is
          and is not
the Scribe who knew the King's spittle.

After the soldier alighted,
a black-bearded, invalid-faced man,
stern as Nathan, head covered,
followed by a fat woman, a tourist
wearing the same Phoenician purple
          as once Bathsheba did,
her jewelled wrist, for one moment,
a drizzle of electric.

But no bizarre crowned phantom
will sign the Register
          at the King David Hotel.

Like the lethargic darkness
of 3000 years ago,
once captive, cornered
within the narrow-windowed
          Temple of Solomon,
everything has vanished into the light.

Except the stones. The stones only.

There is a bazaar-loud haggling
            in the chiaroscuro
            of the alleyways,
tongue-gossip in the gravel walks,
even in the oven of the Squares,
a discontinuous, secret weeping
of a husband or wife, belittled and betrayed
behind the shut door of an unrecorded house.

There is a kissing of the stones,
a kneeling on the stones,
            psalmody and hymnody,
winged prayers swarming in the domed hives
of mosques, synagogues, churches,
ebullitions of harsh religion.

– For thou art my lamp, O Lord . . .
– In the name of God, Lord of the Worlds . . .
– Hear the voice of my supplications . . .
– And forgive us our trespasses . . .
– The Lord is my shepherd I shall not want . . .
– My fortress, my high tower, my deliverer . . .
– The Lord is my shepherd I shall not . . .
            . . . my buckler, my hiding place . . .
– I am poured out like water . . .
– The Lord is my shepherd . . .
            . . . and my bones are vexed . . .
– The Lord is . . .
            – Allah Akbar!
            – Sovereign of the Universe!
            – Our Father in Heaven!

     – Father of Mercies!
     – Shema Yisroael!

There is a tremendous hush in the hills
         above the hills
where the lizard is on the ledges,
where the snake is in the crevices,
after the shadow of an aeroplane
         has hurtled and leapt
below the hills and on to the hills
         that surround Jerusalem.